Painting on Porcelain

Sensational designs for stylish entertaining

Florence de Beaudrap

D&C
David and Charles

A DAVID & CHARLES BOOK

Copyright © by LTA - Meta-Éditions, 2005
Originally published in France as Peinture sur Porcelaine

First published in the UK in 2006 by David & Charles
Reprinted 2007
David & Charles is an F+W Publications Inc. company
4700 East Galbraith Road
Cincinnati, OH 45236

A catalogue record for this book is available from the British Library.

ISBN-13: 978-0-7153-2570-4 paperback
ISBN-10: 0-7153-2570-1 paperback

Printed in China by RR Donnelley
for David & Charles
Brunel House   Newton Abbot   Devon

Visit our website at www.davidandcharles.co.uk

David & Charles books are available from all good bookshops;
alternatively you can contact our Orderline on 0870 9908222 or
write to us at FREEPOST EX2 110, D&C Direct, Newton Abbot, TQ12 4ZZ
(no stamp required UK only); US customers call 800-289-0963 and
Canadian customers call 800-840-5220.

It's funny how life turns out.

Tableware brought ceramics artist Florence de Beaudrap and myself together many years ago. We met at the 'Pot'en ciel' group where we were involved in an extensive project targeted at raising the prospects of the underprivileged.

Pot'en ciel brings together students who are looking to play their part in building a brighter tomorrow. Together they have chosen to support an NGO in Peru which runs a children's home. Bursting with positive energy and complete commitment to their cause, they are currently busy raising funds to help teenagers over there to get into higher education.

Florence and myself are involved, in our different ways, in assisting the young people at Pot'en ciel. They are honest, genuine and determined, and we have absolute faith in them. It is our hope that our collaboration will go some way towards helping them win their battle, however tough it may be along the way.

Jean-Pierre Coffe

Acknowledgements

I would like to thank Jean-Pierre Coffe for his support at Pot'en ciel, Eugène Loridant for his computing wizardry, Benoît, Stanislas, Sybille, Brice, Bérénice, Guylaine and Véronique for their advice and recommendations, and last but by no means least, chef Sébastien Bourgeois for his delicious recipes from the Villa Marinette.

Hand-painted ceramics provide a fantastic opportunity to combine something of artistic beauty with something practical.

This book is about brightening up the little things in life so that each lovingly prepared recipe becomes a precious moment shared between friends. It offers a wide range of themes for tableware to suit all occasions.

Picnics, hot chocolate, children's snacks, fish dishes or game – each occasion has its own special tableware that will not only give you precious memories to treasure forever but will make your food taste even better, too!

It's time to get creative. Enjoy sharing your precious creations.

CONTENTS

Hints and tips

Equipment required

Glass square or tile to use as a palette
Color pigments*
Oily medium (MX54)
Turpentine
Diluting medium

Brushes

Ceradel series 301 no.2, no.5
Raphael series 6240 no.6
Series 652 no.2
Series 6434 no.3
Series 772 no.1, no.4

Pencil for use on enamel
Carbon paper for use on enamel
Sponge
Foam roller
Masking fluid
Spatula
Cocktail sticks
Pen nib and holder
Paper towels
Banding wheel
Masking tape
Acetone or methylated spirits

*The colors mentioned in this book refer to the Schjerning range; other–makes such as Peter–Lavem and Ceradel are also mentioned.

**This involves pricking round the–outline of the design drawn on tracing paper and then dabbing the design with a pad filled with charcoal powder which transfers the pattern on to the porcelain.

Preparing your templates

Before getting started be sure to prepare your motifs carefully as this will make your work much easier.

Make a copy of your motif, or design your own, on a sheet of tracing paper. Place the paper on the surface you want to paint, making sure that it is in the right place and well-centred. Secure with sticky tape.

Slide a sheet of carbon paper between your tracing paper and your surface (dark side against the surface). Go over the design carefully using a ball-point pen.

Note: you can only use your transfer a limited number of times because the outline will start to blur and become less clear.

To make lots of copies you should use a technique known as pouncing**.

Preparing your colors

These products are toxic so you should always work in a well-ventilated space.

Start by wiping down your tile palette with a paper towel to remove colors and dust. Using a spatula, place the required amount of pigment on your tile, add a drop of turpentine and start to gradually work in the medium. Mix together, making sure all the grains of pigment have been completely absorbed and the mix is even. After a short while, check the consistency of your mix. It should be neither too thick nor too thin. Too much medium will make it too thick and too much turpentine will make it too runny and will attract a lot of dust. Have a practice run before you start. The paint should flow easily but not run. You could also add a drop of clove oil or lavender oil to your mix to slow down the drying process.

Using your brushes

Never underestimate the importance of choosing the right brush.

• Long, fine brushes are used for retouching (see below right).

• Flat-ended brushes are used for painting handles, cup lips and wide bands of color.

• Banding brushes are used for working with a banding wheel.

Everyone has their favourite brushes. It is important to take good care of them in order to get the best possible finish.

Always pull your brushstrokes towards you as you work to give yourself maximum control. This will mean that you will, of course, have to turn your work around a lot.

Load your brush evenly. To produce exciting shade effects try loading color on to the side of the brush. Experiment using your brush in different ways to add shape or shading; or keep your color even by stippling with a stippling brush.

Outlining and retouching

There are a number of different techniques for painting on ceramics. My preferred techniques are outlining and retouching.

Outlining: once you have transferred your chosen design on to your piece, work on the outline of the motif, filling in only a little color and shading before the first firing.

Retouching: after the first firing, add more shading to avoid a build-up of color layers. At this stage you can also create interesting transparent effects.

Stippling

Stippling brushes allow you to even out small areas of your brushstrokes and create shade effects. To lay color evenly over larger surface areas, use a sponge stippling pad.

Cover a sponge with a thin layer of foam. Lay the color over the surface to be painted using a wide flat-ended brush, then dab firmly and evenly with the pad. Make your movements lighter as you go, like the bounce of a table tennis ball as it comes to a stop. Now and again, dab off excess paint from your foam pad on to a paper towel. Stippling should be done in thin, even layers. Two firings gives a far better finish.

Serti

Serti is a technique used for outlining motifs to lock in the colors.

Make up your pigments with a resist medium and work them together with a spatula. Using a pen nib, pick up a little of the mix and work around the outline of your design as if you were writing to build up color along the edges.

Banding

Banding can look great on certain pieces. Stripes are made using a banding wheel with a special brush. The hard part is getting your piece in the very centre of the wheel and painting without moving your hand!

It takes a few miles of painting to get used to!

Masking fluid and tape

Pink masking fluid allows you to protect a section of your work so you can go over the edges without ruining your piece.

Use a spatula to pick up a little masking fluid and apply it with a synthetic brush to the areas you want to protect – the centre of a flower, handle edges, etc. After use, always rinse your brush with soap and water.

Once dry, remove the thin skin with a pen. Don't forget to remove it before firing!

Tape works in a similar way for masking straight lines. Make sure you stick the edges down carefully so that no paint seeps underneath.

Tips

To locate the centre of a plate, draw around the base on a sheet of paper. Cut it out and fold your paper into four and this will give you the centre. Cup bases, buttons and other round objects are very useful for drawing circles of different diameters.

Small tools such as a banding guide will help you with your banding. Dividers will help you divide your piece into equal parts. Hand-painted ceramics is a great place to try out new techniques. Why not try experimenting with food wrap or a fan brush for personalized effects?

Firing

Firing temperatures for the colors are between 1472°F and 1580°F. Reds tend to fire at 1382°F. To make life easier for yourself, make a habit of putting the more delicate colors at the bottom of the kiln and others higher up. The best way to master firing is simply through trial and error. You can be sure that pleasant – and not-so-pleasant – surprises lie in store!

Snowflakes

Transport yourself to snow-capped peaks with snowflake motifs on warming red, and patterns inspired by France's Haute Savoie region.

Brandy mocha

2 FL OZ BRANDY
1 TSP SUGAR
8 FL OZ COFFEE
8 FL OZ HOT CHOCOLATE
6 TBSP DOUBLE CREAM
GRATED CHOCOLATE

● Combine together the hot chocolate, coffee, brandy and sugar in a pan over a low heat. Do not boil. Pour into mugs. Whip the cream and place on top. Finish with a sprinkling of grated chocolate.

Templates on page 88

Color

Iron red

Mug

1. Use tape to mask off a strip around the top of the mug for the heart pattern.

Stipple the rest of the mug in red with a sponge. Allow to dry completely (this should take 24 to 48–hours). Remove the tape and clean your mug.

2. Once the paint is completely dry, etch the snowflakes freehand using a cocktail stick. Dust off any flakes of paint on the mug.

First firing.

3. Transfer the heart pattern on to the mug and paint it in iron red using a medium brush. Start and finish the pattern each side of the handle.

Second firing.

TIPS

Make sure your stippling is completely dry before adding the snowflakes so that you can handle the mug easily, taking care not to scratch it. Practise drawing snowflakes on a tile first.

Espresso cup

1. Stipple color all over the cup except for the handle. Leave to dry as for the mug.

2. When the paint is completely dry, etch the snowflakes into the paint with a cocktail stick. Wipe off any flakes of paint.

Fire.

Saucer

1. Mask off the centre of the saucer with tape leaving space in the middle to draw a snowflake with a pen nib.

2. Stipple around the edge of the saucer and remove the tape. Clean.

Fire.

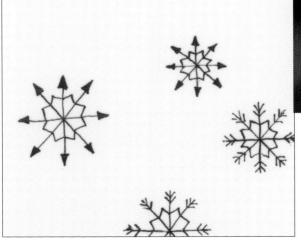

Winter scenes

This deliciously warming French recipe offers welcome relief from wintry snowflakes and ice!

Tartiflette

FEEDS 8
$2^1/_4$ LB POTATOES, DICED
1 REBLOCHON CHEESE
1 ONION
$3^1/_2$ OZ LARDONS OR BACON BITS
SALT AND PEPPER

● Gently fry the onion and bacon in a pan. When the onion is golden brown add the diced potatoes and continue to fry with a little salt and pepper. Transfer the mix to an ovenproof dish. Slice the Reblochon cheese lengthways and position crust-upwards. Bake. Serve hot when the Reblochon has melted over the potatoes.

Templates on pages 88 and 89

Colors

Dark blue

Ceradel midnight blue

Border brown

Brown red

Black

Ceradel olive green

Ivory yellow

Dinner plate

1. Transfer the central motif on to your plate (see pages 88-89 for templates). Stick a length of tape around the inner edge of the plate rim. Paint the design, building up the colors and paying special attention to shape and shading. At this stage your design should be very delicately painted.

2. Stipple the outer section of the plate in dark blue with a little flux added. Remove the tape and clean. **First firing.**

3. Retouch the central motif, focusing on shading and going over the original outlines in a darker shade. The snow, which is blue to contrast with the white of the plate, should be left light and clear.

4. Add a pinch of midnight blue to the dark blue and, using a banding wheel, paint fine lines either side of your stippling on the rim. **Second firing.**

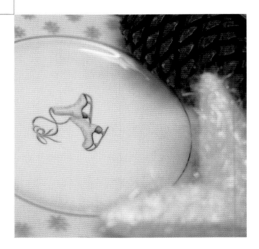

Colors

Dark blue

Ceradel olive green

Border brown

Brown red

Black

Side plate

1. Transfer the central motif on to your plate (see page 89 for templates). As for the dinner plate, paint the outlines very lightly.

2. Mark where the lines will go on the plate rim with a pencil. Using a pen nib, add snowflakes around the edge in dark blue.

First firing.

3. Add shading to the motif by using darker colors. Add fine lines on the rim using a banding wheel as for the dinner plate.

Second firing.

Cup

1. Make a trace of the wavy line (see page 88 for template) and transfer on to your cup about 1in from the lip. Paint masking fluid below the line and down the sides of the handle. In the same way as for the side plate, use a pen nib to add snowflakes. Add a snowflake inside the cup, too.

2. Stipple the top of the cup in dark blue. Leave to dry. Remove the masking fluid. Clean.

First firing.

3. Go over the edge of the wavy line in dark blue darkened with a pinch of black.

Saucer

Follow the same technique as for the cup.

Wild grasses

A bohemian dish inspired
by wild grasses.

Templates on pages 90, 91, 92 and 93

Wild spring salad

Recipe courtesy of Sébastien Bourgeois
at the Villa Marinette

1LB ROCKET

4 ROSES (UNSPRAYED)

12 NASTURTIUM FLOWERS

12 PANSIES

1 BUNCH BASIL

CHIVES

PARSLEY

BALSAMIC VINEGAR

OLIVE OIL

SALT AND PEPPER

PARMESAN CHEESE

● Remove the petals from the roses and rinse in cold water with the rocket, basil, chives, parsley and the other flowers. Drain gently. Make up your dressing and pour over the salad, then toss. Top with shavings of parmesan made using a vegetable peeler.

Wild flower plate

Plate 1

Colors

Grass green	Dark blue
Copenhagen green	Iron red
Rose purple	Black
Carmine	Carmine purple
Albert yellow deep	Terre sienna

Plate 1

1. Transfer the design for plate 1 on to your piece using the template on page 90. Paint the stems and long leaves first using a long, fine brush. Next, go over the thicker leaves, adding curves with a thicker brush. Use an eraser on the outlines.

2. Add the flowers, making sure that you paint from the centre of the flower towards the outside.

3. Lastly, paint a ladybird on the edge of the plate and another on a leaf.

First firing.

4. With a fine brush, create a shading effect by darkening your original colors. Add a little black to the blue and green, add some sienna and green to the yellow and carmine purple to the rose. Go over the veining on the leaves.

5. To finish, paint a green line around the outer edge of the plate.

Second firing.

Colors

Grass green

Copenhagen green

Albert yellow

Rose purple

Dark blue

Ivory yellow

Black

Terre sienna

Iron red

Plate 2

Plate 2

1. Work in the same way as for plate 1, left, using the template on page 91. Start by painting a faint outline and use an eraser if necessary.

2. Next, paint on your flowers. Use ivory yellow for the campion for a great transparent effect.

3. Paint ladybirds in a few different positions on the plate.

First firing.

4. Work in the same way as for plate 1, adding color to the campion with sienna and a few spots of iron red.

5. Add a green line round the edge of the plate.

Second firing.

Plate 3

Plate 3

1. Work in the same way as for plates 1 and 2, transferring the design from page 92 on to your plate. Paint each leaf and flower carefully, paying special attention to their shapes and curves. Paint the ladybirds in iron red and black.

First firing.

2. Go over the stems in grass green and black to add some shading. Add some grey to the daisies to bring them out and some sienna to their centres. Outline the buttercups in green and the bindweed in blue. Finish by painting the edge of the plate in green.

Second firing.

Colors

Grass green	Black
Dark blue	Iron red
Ivory yellow	Albert yellow
Grey for flowers	

Meadow frieze plate

1. Transfer the grass design and ladybird on to your plate using the template on page 93. Go over the grass with a long, fine brush, starting at the top of each blade and painting down towards the base. Using a thick brush, apply color to the green area and even it out quickly with a sponge. Working in the same way as for the previous wild flower plates, paint the flowers and ladybird. Wipe off any imperfections.

First firing.

2. Retouch the flowers and paint the edge as before.

Second firing.

Citrus fun

These bright, fruit-decorated dishes are ideal for fun-filled desserts.

Templates on page 94

Strawberry Bavarois

1LB 10OZ STRAWBERRIES
3/4 CUP SUGAR
2 THICK YOGHURTS
HALF A LEMON
1 CUP CREAM
8 GELATINE SHEETS
1 TBSP OIL

● Soften the gelatine in cold water. Whip 2 tbsp cream. Blend 1lb strawberries to make a coulis. Add the sugar, lemon and yoghurt. Heat the remaining cream and add the gelatine and strawberry purée. Allow to cool and then add the whipped cream. Oil a loaf tin. Cut the left over strawberries into thin slices and add them to the mix. Pour carefully into the tin and leave to set in the refrigerator for at least 12 hours.

Colors

Sepia brown

Albert yellow deep

Terre sienna

Ceradel olive green

Peter Lavem orange red

Peter Lavem antique gold

Black

Yellow green

Dessert plates

Strawberry and cherry

1. Transfer the templates from page 94. Use red to fill in the cherries and strawberries, leaving a small 'comma' shape to give the illusion of light on the cherries. Do the same with the seeds on the strawberries. Paint the leaves, collars and hats in olive green, adding shading as you work. Paint the faces in antique gold and pink.

Paint the arms and legs in sepia brown with a long, fine brush. Add some hair. Using a pen nib, write in French (or English) just below the rim. Mark the position of the pattern around the rim of the plate and then paint the fruits. Paint the wavy pattern around the edge of the plate in yellow.

First firing at 1472°F at the bottom of the kiln.

2. Paint masking fluid over the fruits, edging and lettering you have painted.

Mask off strips with tape and stipple between them in yellow green.

Remove the tape and clean the plate. Retouch the fruits to accentuate the shading.

Second firing at 1472°F at the bottom of the kiln.

Tomber dans les pommes

Pressé comme un citron

Ramener sa fraise

Rouge comme une cerise

Apples and lemon

1. Work in the same way as for the strawberry and cherry plates. Paint the leaves in olive green and the legs, arms and hair as before. Add the lettering with a pen nib.

2. Outline the apples and lemon in Albert yellow, leaving a section white to give the illusion of a reflection. Paint the wavy pattern around the edge of the plate in red.

First firing at 1472°F at the bottom of the kiln.

3. Paint masking fluid over the fruits, edging and lettering. Prepare strips using masking tape and stipple yellow green between them. Leave to dry and clean. Retouch the fruits, adding sienna to the yellow and a little green to the lemon.

Second firing at 1472°F at the bottom of the kiln.

Cups

Use the same technique to decorate the cups.

All at sea

Nautical-themed tableware for your beach house.

Monkfish surprise

1³/₄ LB MONKFISH FILLETS
4 EGGS
1 SMALL TIN TOMATO PURÉE
¹/₂ CUP CRÈME FRAÎCHE
1 TSP CORNFLOUR

● Poach the monkfish in a court-bouillon. Drain and leave to cool. Mix together the tomato purée and crème fraîche. Beat the eggs as if making an omelette. Add salt and pepper to taste. Fold the cornflour into the eggs and add the crème fraîche and tomato purée. Place the monkfish fillets in a greased dish, pour on the egg mix and bake in a bain marie for about 35 minutes. Serve cold with mayonnaise.

Templates on pages 95 and 96

Dinner plate

1. Transfer a boat, lighthouse or beach hut motif into the centre of each plate.

2. Draw the outline of each motif. Paint the boat sails in border brown and stipple hard to make them look lightweight.

Paint the boat hulls in grey and red and outline the beach hut in grey with a red outline for the door. Paint the lighthouse in grey and add a red top. Don't forget to add the railings in black using a very fine brush.

3. Using a pencil, draw two lines around the rim of the plate $1/2$ in apart. Trace the ring at the top of the plate. Paint the rope freehand around the plate, keeping between the two lines you have drawn, using light blue. Paint the ring in border brown.

First firing.

4. After firing, go over the outlines to bring out the shading and contrast. Go over the rope pattern in dark blue.

Second firing.

TIPS

The rope pattern requires a special brush technique that gives you a curve.

The technique takes a little practise but is easy to pick up.

Colors
Light blue
Grey for flowers
Dark blue
Black
Border brown
Iron red

Side plate

Use the same colors as for the dinner plate.

1. Divide the edge of the plate into eight sections. (see page 95 for template). You should have four large sections, painted blue with 4 smaller white sections between them.

2. Paint masking fluid each side of the blue sections. Transfer the rope motif on to the plate.

3. Stipple the blue sections in light blue, making the sides darker and the centre lighter to give the impression of a rounded lifebelt. Paint the rope in border brown working in the same way as for the dinner plate. Remove the masking fluid and clean.

First firing.

4. Shade the white sections with a little grey to give the impression of light reflecting off the lifebelt all around the plate. Finish the rope in border brown mixed with a little black. Finally, using a long, fine brush, add the red lines.

Second firing.

> **Colors**
> Albert yellow deep
> Light blue
> Dark blue
> Iron red
> Border brown
> Black

Bowls

1. Transfer the motifs on to the inside of the bowls and paint them lightly, finishing with the small rope motif.

2. Transfer the rope pattern on to the outside of the bowls in light blue, incorporating your chosen name into the motif.

First firing.

3. Paint masking fluid over the motifs inside the bowls. Stipple in light blue. Remove the masking fluid. Leave to dry. Add some shading to the rope and the motif inside the bowls.

Second firing.

Milk jug

You could explore this theme further on all sorts of tableware. Why not personalize your work by adding an inscription, a picture of your family boat, something to remind you of your favourite beach or a beach hut number?

Wrought iron

Eat out on the deck or veranda with friends using this set with an outdoor wrought-iron theme.

Rabbit terrine

1 RABBIT
3 SHALLOTS
7OZ SMOKED LARDONS OR BACON BITS
THYME, BAY LEAF, SALT AND PEPPER
WHITE WINE (CHABLIS)
1 TBSP OIL

● The night before, place the rabbit in a terrine with the diced shallots and lardons in layers. Add the bay leaf, thyme, and salt and pepper and cover with the oil and white wine. Leave to marinate overnight. The next morning, cook in an oven for–approximately 1 hour 30–minutes. Keep moist. Serve hot with steamed potatoes or–rice.

Templates on pages 97, 98 and 99

Dinner plate

1. Divide the plate (shown below) into five and mask off, with tape, the edges of the sections that will be marbled.

2. Marbling

Make up some grey, for flowers, and rose purple. Using a sponge, apply the two colors unevenly, working diagonally to create a veining effect. With a clean and dry, medium-sized brush, go over the veins, bringing your brush up at a different angle every time. Each section of marbling is different so add more or fewer veins to suit your taste. Finally, add some grey to the veins in a few areas and bring out some of the veins with a pen. Remove the tape and wipe off any imperfections.

First firing.

3. Copy the wrought iron motifs and the chairs on to the plate. Paint over each wrought iron design in black using a fine brush. Leave to dry. Add some shading to the chairs in grey.

Second firing.

Colors

Rose purple
Grey for flowers
Black

Side plate

1. Transfer the patterns on page 98 or 99 and the central motifs on to your plates (shown left) and paint them in black.

First firing.

2. Paint masking fluid on to the motifs, and work as for the dinner plate to paint the marbling around the outside. Leave to dry, then wipe clean.

Second firing.

> **TIPS**
> If you apply the marbling on to all your plates at the same time you can use the same mix, giving you similar colors on the plates after firing.

Bridge

Jacks, queens and kings from this sophisticated card game. Watch out for the joker in the sugar bowl!

Brownies

3 EGGS
1³/₄ STICKS BUTTER
¹/₂ CUP FLOUR
³/₄ CUP SUGAR
7oz CHOCOLATE
CINNAMON

● Melt the chocolate. Melt the butter separately and mix with the sugar and cinnamon. Add the beaten eggs and flour alternately, little by little, and then add the melted chocolate. Grease and flour a tin, pour in the mixture, and bake at 300°F for about 25 minutes.

Templates on pages 100 and 101

Colors

Grass green

White

Peter Lavem crimson

Cyclamen

Border brown

Antique gold

Light blue

Albert yellow deep

Dessert plates

1. Transfer the jacks, queens and kings on to the centre of the plates. Paint the outlines carefully, paying particular attention to the faces.

Paint the queen of diamonds in cyclamen and grass green and the queen of clubs in Albert yellow and light blue.

Paint the jack in cyclamen and grass green and the king of hearts in Albert yellow and light blue. Outline the faces in antique gold with a hint of crimson, and the hair in border brown.

First firing.

2. Transfer the heart or diamond frame motif on to the plate. Go over the clothes, adding shading and details such as stripes, dots and flowers on the fabric. Add some brown to the faces.

3. Add gold to the clothes, crowns, and clubs.

Second firing.

4. Use masking fluid to protect the centre of the plate. Stipple the outside using a different color for each jack, king or queen. Clean and leave to dry. To finish, paint the edge of the central frame in gold.

Third firing.

Use a fibreglass brush to polish the gold. A second coat of gold may be required.

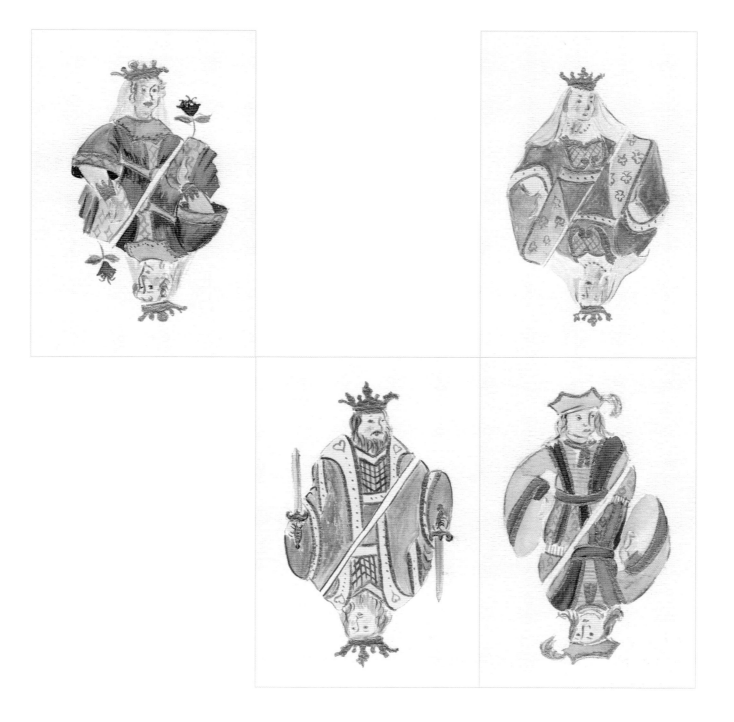

Colors

Light blue

Albert yellow deep

Grass green

Cyclamen

Antique gold

Cups

1. Prepare a different color for each cup. Stipple the outside of the cups and saucers.

2. Clean and leave to dry. Using a banding wheel, paint a line around the inside of the cup and down the handle.

First firing.

3. Transfer the motifs on to the cup. Paint them gold, taking care not to go over the lines because gold leaves behind dark purple lines when fired.

4. Paint a gold line carefully around the edge of the saucer.

Second firing.

Fire at 1436°F because you have used gold on top of color.

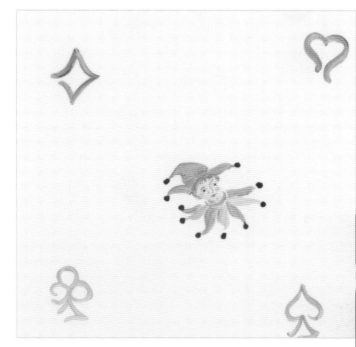

Colors

Grass green

Cyclamen

Border brown

Antique gold

Light blue

Albert yellow deep

Sugar bowl

1. Transfer the joker on to the centre of the sugar bowl. Place hearts, clubs, diamonds and spades over the sugar bowl. Paint the outline of the joker, in the same way as for the plates, using four colors for his costume.

2. Paint each motif in a different color. Paint the bells, frame for the joker and the knob of the sugar bowl in gold.

First firing.

3. Add some shading to the joker's face.

Second firing.

Gingerbread

Enjoy tasty gingerbread treats on this tea set.

Gingerbread

1 CUP BUCKWHEAT AND RYE FLOUR
$^1/_2$ CUP BOILED MILK
2 CUPS WHEAT FLOUR
1 TSP BUTTER
$^3/_4$ CUP DARK CLEAR HONEY
1 EGG (BEATEN)
$^1/_2$ TBSP CARAMEL
1 SACHET VANILLA SUGAR/FEW DROPS
VANILLA ESSENCE
3 CLOVES

● Mix together the flour, caramel and vanilla sugar or essence. Fold the honey into the warm milk. Make a well in the centre of your flour and pour in half the honey and the beaten egg. Mix together and add the rest of the honey little by little until you have an even paste. Pour into a greased loaf tin and bake for about 50–minutes at 375°F, until golden brown.

Templates on page-102

Colors

Terre sienna	Grass green
Chocolate brown	Iron red
Border brown	Flux
Grey for flowers	**Background**
Rose	Ivory yellow
White	Yellow brown

Biscuit tray

1. Transfer the biscuit designs on to the tray. Paint and stipple them in sienna and a little brown.

2. Paint the round biscuits in rose. To paint the green biscuit make up some grass green pigment with $^1/_2$ flux and $^1/_2$ white. Paint and stipple. Paint the sticks of barley sugar in iron red. To finish, paint the heart in border brown.

First firing.

3. Go over the gingerbread motifs in chocolate brown to add some shading, eyes and buttons. Do the same for the brown biscuits. Decorate the rose biscuits with red and the green biscuits with brown. To finish, use grey to add some shading to the white parts on the barley sugar sticks.

Second firing.

4. Paint masking fluid over all the biscuits. Leave to dry. Lay ivory yellow over the entire surface of the tray with a relatively fine brush. Immediately afterwards, brush on yellow brown in some areas. Stipple with a sponge. Some areas will be lighter than others.

5. To finish, crumple up a sheet of food wrap and place it over the fresh paint to create a texture similar to that of rag painting. Leave to dry. Remove the masking fluid and clean.

Third firing.

Colors

Terre sienna

Chocolate brown

Border brown

Grey for flowers

Background

Ivory yellow

Yellow brown

Plates

1. Use masking tape or paint some masking fluid around the inside rim of the plate. Transfer the gingerbread motifs on to the centre of the plate.

2. Paint the biscuits in sienna in the same way as for the biscuit tray.

3. Paint and stipple the plate rim in the same way as the tray surface. Remove the tape or masking fluid and clean.

First firing.

4. Go over the different shapes in chocolate brown and border brown to add shade and outline. Finish off with some grey for flowers.

5. Lastly, using a round brush, paint small dots in chocolate brown around the inside edge of the plate rim.

Second firing.

Leaves

Beautiful green leaves at the height of summer complement a warm mushroom pâté.

Warm mushroom pâté

Courtesy of Sébastien Bourgeois at the Villa Marinette

$2^{1}/_{4}$ LB MUSHROOMS
$1^{3}/_{4}$ OZ GARLIC
$3^{1}/_{2}$ OZ SHALLOTS
4 CUPS DOUBLE CREAM
10 EGGS
1 BUNCH PARSLEY (CHOPPED)

● Wash the mushrooms and slice into small chunks. Fry them in some oil with the chopped shallots. Pour in the cream, beaten eggs and parsley and season. Pour the mix into greased individual ramekins and place in the oven in a bain marie for 40 minutes at 325°F.

Templates on page 103

Colors

Grass green

Yellow green

Albert yellow deep

Sepia brown

Black

Dinner plate

1. Transfer the six leaves on to the plates, one per plate. Paint masking fluid around the outside of each leaf. Mix up yellow, the two greens and sepia brown on your palette.

Using a fairly wide brush, apply the color in layers, starting with yellow, then moving to yellow green and finally grass green.

2. Using a wide-tipped stippling brush or even a sponge, stipple the three colors to blend them together to obtain a nice graduated effect. Finish with the stem, painted with a single brushstroke in sepia brown.

Remove the masking fluid and clean.

First firing.

3. Add black to the grass green and add veins to each leaf using a long, fine brush.

4. Use the same color to paint the outline of each leaf for extra shading.

Add a little black to the brown and add shading to one side of the stem.

5. Finish off by painting a line around the inside of–the rim of the dinner plate and around the outside of the side plate.

Second firing.

Fly fishing

These dazzling colors will make your fish dishes the freshest of the fresh.

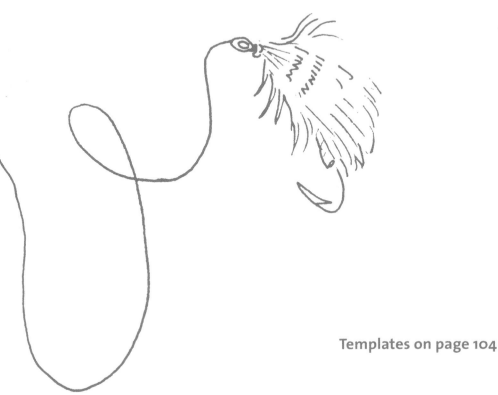

Templates on page 104

Trout with a watercress sauce

1 BUNCH WATERCRESS
1 STICK BUTTER
4 TROUT FILLETS
1 CUP DOUBLE CREAM
2 TOMATOES (DICED)
1 CUP WHITE WINE
3 TBSP OIL
2 SHALLOTS (CHOPPED)
SALT
PEPPER

● Fry the shallots gently in some butter, add the wine and reduce. Add the cream and bring to the boil for two minutes. Fold in the rest of the butter and then add the finely chopped watercress, salt and pepper.
Heat for one minute. Stir together and strain. In a pan, brown the trout fillets in some oil. Serve with a drizzling of sauce. Garnish with a couple of watercress leaves and some diced tomatoes.

Fish-themed tableware

Serving dish

1. Transfer the fish hooks on to the dish. Paint the hooks black. Paint each fly delicately in the colors of your choice using a fine brush.

First firing.

2. Go over each fly again to bring out the colors. Add a little black to some of them. Finish with a line in wood brown around the edge of the dish.

Second firing.

Colors

Grey for flowers
Light blue
Black
Iron red
Wood brown
Moss green
Canary yellow
Delfter blue
Border brown

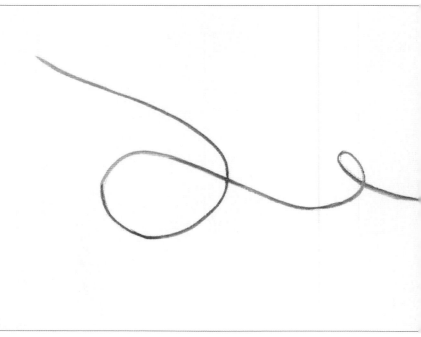

Dinner plate

1. Transfer a hook on to the rim of the plate. Paint the hook in black and the fly in color.

First firing.

2. Go over the fly in the same way as for the serving dish. Using a banding wheel, paint a line that goes round the rim and through the fly hook ring using wood brown.

Second firing.

Side plate

Transfer the fishing rod on to the rim of the plate and paint.

With a very long, fine brush, paint the line in a single stroke. Paint the hook and fly in the same way as for the dinner plate.

First firing.

Retouch as before.

Second firing.

Carousel

The dazzling array of colors on this carousel set is sure to turn heads!

Fruit carousel tart

2 CUPS FLOUR

1 STICK BUTTER

1 EGG

$1^3/_4$ OZ SUGAR

PINCH SALT

7OZ BLACKBERRIES

7OZ STRAWBERRIES

7OZ RASPBERRIES

2 KIWI FRUIT

REDCURRANT JAM

1 TBSP VANILLA SUGAR/FEW DROPS VANILLA ESSENCE

● Make a sugar crust pastry case using the ingredients above and bake. Cover the base with redcurrant jam. Fill one quarter of the tart with strawberries, another with blackberries, then raspberries and finally kiwi fruit. Serve immediately.

Templates on pages 105, 106 and 107

Colors

Canary yellow

Iron red

Grey for flowers

Grass green

Dark blue

Black

Terre sienna

Border brown

Teacup

1. Transfer the motifs on to the cups, adapting the size of the upper border to suit your pieces.

With a pen nib, outline the motifs and the carousel structure in black.

First firing.

2. Use tape to mask off round the base of the cup. Stipple in yellow, remove tape and clean.

Add shading to the animals and vehicles in grey, making some sides darker to give the impression of three dimensions.

3. Add extra shading to the horse's mane and tail with a little black.

Now add the other colors. Filling in the colors is a fairly tricky process. Shade sections of the poles in grey and others in iron red to match the top edge of

the cup. Finish with the kitten hiding behind one of the poles and the cord with a tassel painted in sienna and border brown.

Second firing.

Saucer

1. Transfer the edge pattern on to the saucer, $^{1}/_{2}$in from the edge, adapting it to fit your piece. Go around the outline in black with a pen nib.

First firing.

2. Paint masking fluid over the edge pattern and around the centre of the saucer, leaving the section to be painted yellow. Leave to dry. Stipple in canary yellow. Remove the masking fluid and clean.

Second firing.

3. Now paint masking fluid on the yellow section and stipple the edge in red. Remove the masking fluid and clean.

Third firing.

Colors

Canary yellow

Iron red

Grey for flowers

Grass green

Dark blue

Border brown

Terre sienna

Black

Tart dish

1. Enlarge or reduce the motif to fit your dish.

Ensure that the motif is well centred and transfer it on to the dish. Add animals and vehicles and outline in black.

First firing.

2. Using masking fluid in the same way as for the saucer, stipple the centre in yellow, then stipple around it in red without going over the yellow. Mask off the dish edge with some tape. Stipple in yellow. Remove the masking fluid and tape and clean carefully. Leave to dry.

3. Repeat the same steps as for the figures on the teacup, taking care not to run into the outer yellow edge.

Second firing.

TIPS

For extra protection fire again after painting the edge of your dish.

67

The hunt

Swap tales of the great outdoors over this delightful dinner set.

Haunch of venison with shallots

1 HAUNCH VENISON
8 SHALLOTS
BUTTER
1 CUP DOUBLE CREAM
SALT
PEPPER
2 SUGAR CUBES

● Cook the venison in a few knobs of butter in a pre-heated oven. Baste frequently and add your chopped shallots. Once cooked, carve the meat and keep warm. Drain off the jus and shallots into a pan and heat, adding the cream and sugar. Drizzle the sauce over the venison and serve straight away with a celeriac purée.

Templates on pages 108, 109 and 110

Colors
Chestnut brown
Black
Iron red

Dinner plate

1. Transfer one of the hound motifs on to the dinner plate and one of the prey animals on to the plate edge. The appropriate tracks should go from the hounds in the direction of the animal. Use a pen nib to draw the outline of the hounds, prey and tracks.

First firing.

2. Add chestnut brown shading to the animals using a stippling brush. Fill in the tracks. Use a banding wheel to add a line in iron red all the way around the edge of the plate, excluding where the animals are painted.

Second firing.

Side plate

1. Transfer the animal portraits and their frames on to the plates and outline in chestnut brown. Leave to dry or fire.

First firing.

2. Shade in each animal in the same way as for the dinner plate. Paint shading on the left side in grey. Fill in the frames using chestnut brown.

Second firing.

3. Paint masking fluid over the frame. Stipple the outside of the plate in iron red. Remove masking fluid and clean.

Third firing.

Colors

Chestnut brown

Grey for flowers

Iron red

Chandeliers

Perfect for brightening
up your afternoon tea!

Pink biscuit fondant cake

1¼ STICKS BUTTER
24 PINK RHEIMS BISCUITS
3 EGG YOLKS
3 TBSP RUM OR COINTREAU
1¼ CUP SUGAR
ICING:
4½ OZ CHOCOLATE
½ STICK BUTTER

● Soften the sticks of butter and add the egg yolks, sugar and alcohol. Break down the biscuits into breadcrumbs and add to the mix. Pour into a greased tin. To make the icing, melt the chocolate with the butter and spread over the cake. Chill for at least two–hours. Remove from the tin.

Templates on page 111

74

White teacup

1. Transfer the motifs on to the cup.

Paint the chandeliers in violet or carmine using a fine brush.

Add a candlestick inside the cup, too.

2. Paint the edge of the handle and round the lip of the cup with a flat-ended brush.

First firing.

3. Paint gold on to parts of the chandeliers. Paint gold dots around the lip of the cup and the sides of the handle.

Second firing.

Matching saucer

1. Paint masking fluid on to the saucer to mask off the edges, following the relief of the saucer. Stipple the remainder in violet or carmine. Remove the masking fluid and clean.

First firing.

2. Add some gold dots along the edge of the color.

Second firing.

Colors

Violet

Carmine

Black

Gold

Colored teacup

1. Stipple the outside of the cup and the outside flat edge of the handle in violet or carmine. Make sure your background color is not too dark or you will have problems tracing on to it.

First firing.

2. Transfer the chandelier motifs on to the cup. Paint the chandelier motifs in gold. Add a candlestick on the inside of the mug. Paint gold dots round the edges of the handle.

Second firing at 1436°F because you have applied gold over the color.

3. Use a pen nib to carfully re-outline parts of the chandeliers in black.

Third firing at 1436°F.

Matching saucer

1. Reversing the technique of the previous saucer, paint masking fluid on to the inside of the saucer, following its outline. Stipple in violet or carmine around the edge of the saucer. Leave to dry, remove the masking fluid and clean.

2. Add gold dots outside the edge of the color.

First firing.

Colors

Lilac

Carmine

Gold

Large dish

1. Stipple the outside of the dish in lilac. Leave to dry. Stipple the inside in carmine.

First firing.

2. Transfer the delicate stars on to the dish. Concentrate them in the centre of the base of the dish, spacing them out as you move towards the sides.

Paint them gold, starting in the centre. Finish by painting a gold band around the top edge.

Second firing at 1436°F.

Flowers

The freshness and vibrancy of this dinner set makes it perfect for a light lunch.

Open summer sandwich

1 LARGE SLICE OF SOURDOUGH LOAF PER PERSON
MIXED SEASONED SALAD
AUBERGINE CAVIAR
BACON
SHREDDED CHICKEN BREAST
TOMATOES
BASIL
FROMAGE FRAIS
SALT AND PEPPER

● Fry the pieces of chicken and bacon. Toast the slices of bread. Place the seasoned salad on a dinner plate with tomato quarters and a little chopped basil on the side. Spread the aubergine caviar on to the bread and lay the chicken and bacon on top. Place on top of the salad. Add a generous spoonful of fromage frais on to the side of the plate and season to taste.

Templates on page 112

Colors

Ceradel rose purple

Peter Lavem purple

Peter Lavem grass green

Ceradel orange

White

Relief white

Dinner plate

1. Stick tapes of different widths and lengths on to the plate as shown, then remove every other one. Paint between the tapes, alternating the colors as you go. Remove the remaining tapes and clean.

First firing.

2. This time place masking tape strips on the bands you have already painted and paint the remaining spaces. Remove the tapes and clean.

Second firing.

3. Use tape and masking fluid to mask off all the painted stripes.

Stipple the rest of the plate in grass green mixed with some white. Remove tapes and masking fluid and clean.

Third firing.

TIPS

Use the same technique using masking strips to paint the knife rest.

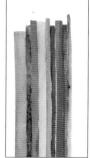

Small bowl

1. Draw the petals on to the bowl. Paint them in rose purple with a thick brush to achieve a veined effect.

Take a cocktail stick and, starting at the centre, etch deeper veins in the petals.

First firing.

2. Outline the petals in purple. Go over the veins again, this time with a long, fine brush, painting grass green into the centre of the veins.

3. Prepare grass green, orange, rose and white with some relief white. Mix each color into a thick paste. Use a cocktail stick or a brush to dab spots into the centre of the flower.

Second firing.

4. Paint masking fluid over the edges of the petals and stipple grass green leaves with a hint of white between each one. Remove the masking fluid and add a touch of dark rose to the edges of some of the petals.

Third firing.

Useful addresses

Tableware, equipment and materials for ceramics

Rynne China
222 West Eight Mile Road,
Hazel Park,
Michigan, 48030
Tel. (248) 542-9400
Catalogue and mail order
www.rynnechina.com
E-mail: info@rynnechina.com

Tableware, paints, equipment and materials for ceramics

TCC Porcelain: The China Corner
Windchimes Shopping Center
13155 Westheimer Road
Houston
Texas, 770077
Tel. (+1) 888 933 2648
Catalogue and mail order
www.peterlavem.com
E-mail: sales@tccporcelain.com

Villa Marinette
Hotel & restaurant
20, avenue du Général-de-Gaulle
78125 Gazeran
France
Tel. +33 (0)1 34 83 19 01

Schjernings Farver A/S
Østeralle 21,
Postboks 119,
8400 Ebeltoft,
Denmark
Tel. (+45) 86-34-22-11
www.schjernings-farver.com

Ceradel Socor
19-25 rue Frederic Bastiat,
BP 1598,
87022 Limoges,
France
Tel. (+33) 5-55-35-02-35
www.ceradel.com

Templates

SNOWFLAKES:
Mug (page 14)

WINTER SCENES:
Dinner plate (page 18)

SNOWFLAKES:
Espresso cup (page 15)

SNOWFLAKES:
Espresso cup (page 15)

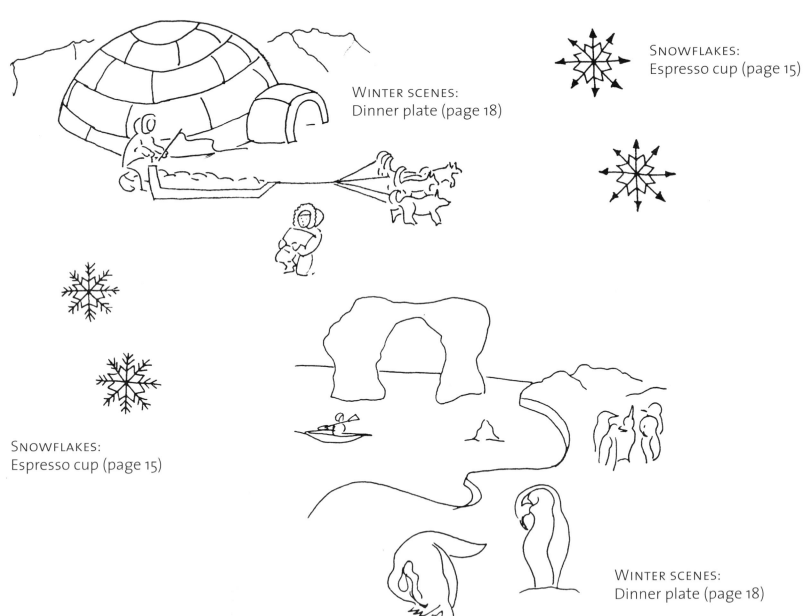

WINTER SCENES:
Dinner plate (page 18)

WINTER SCENES:
Dinner plate (page 18)

WINTER SCENES:
Dinner plate (page 18)

WINTER SCENES:
Side plate (page 20)

WINTER SCENES:
Side plate (page 20)

WILD GRASSES:
Wild flower plate 1 (page 24)

WILD GRASSES:
Wild flower plate 2 (page 25)

WILD GRASSES:
Wild flower plate 3 (page 26)

WILD GRASSES:
Meadow frieze plate (page 27)

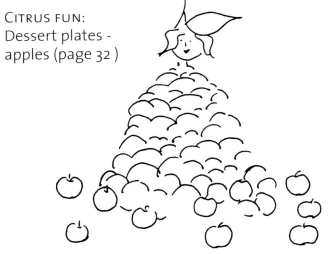

CITRUS FUN:
Dessert plates -
lemon (page 32)

CITRUS FUN:
Dessert plates -
cherry (page31)

CITRUS FUN:
Dessert plates -
apples (page 32)

CITRUS FUN:
Dessert plates -
strawberry (page 31)

CITRUS FUN:
Cups (page 32)

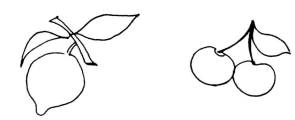

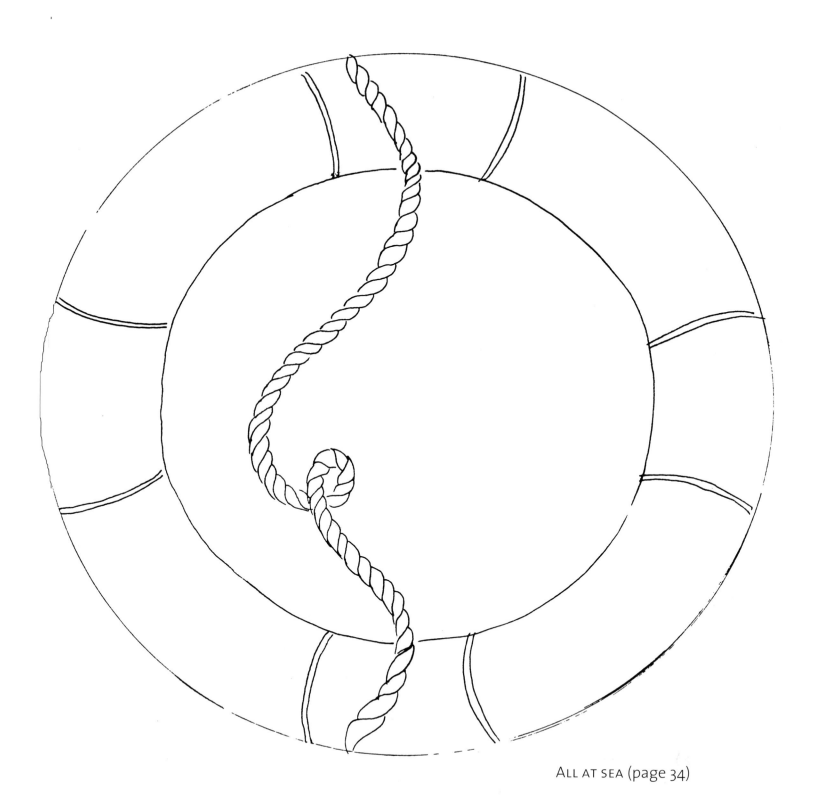

ALL AT SEA (page 34)

ALL AT SEA
(pages 34-39)

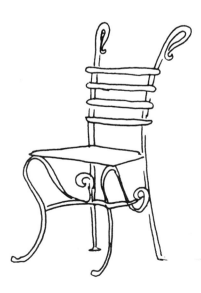

Wrought iron:
Dinner plate (page 42)

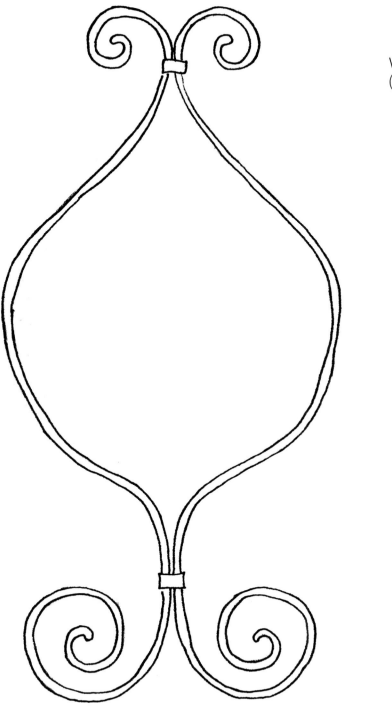

WROUGHT IRON:
(pages 40-43)

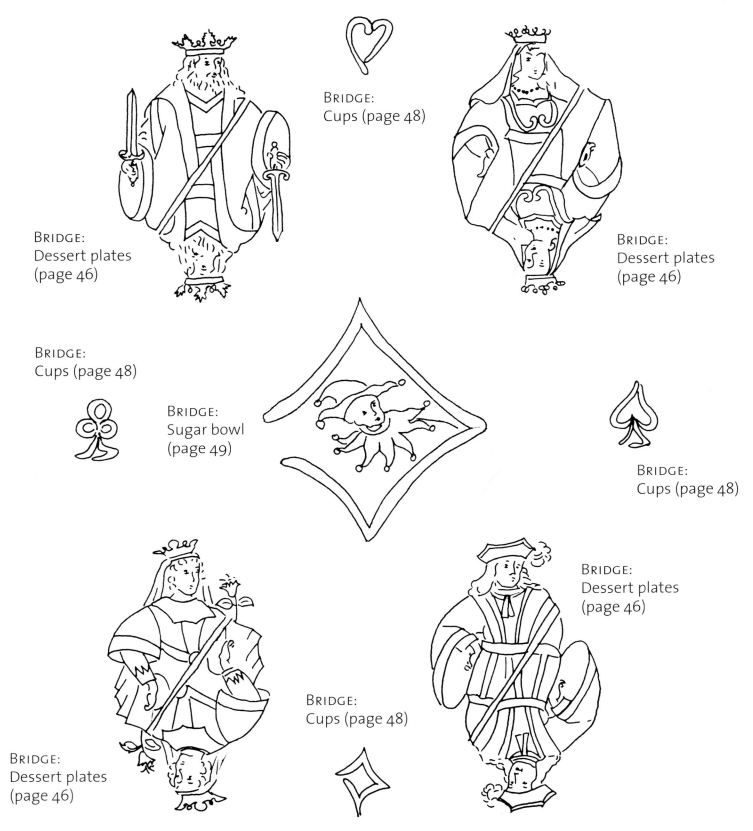

BRIDGE:
Cups (page 48)

BRIDGE:
Dessert plates
(page 46)

BRIDGE:
Dessert plates
(page 46)

BRIDGE:
Cups (page 48)

BRIDGE:
Sugar bowl
(page 49)

BRIDGE:
Cups (page 48)

BRIDGE:
Dessert plates
(page 46)

BRIDGE:
Cups (page 48)

BRIDGE:
Dessert plates
(page 46)

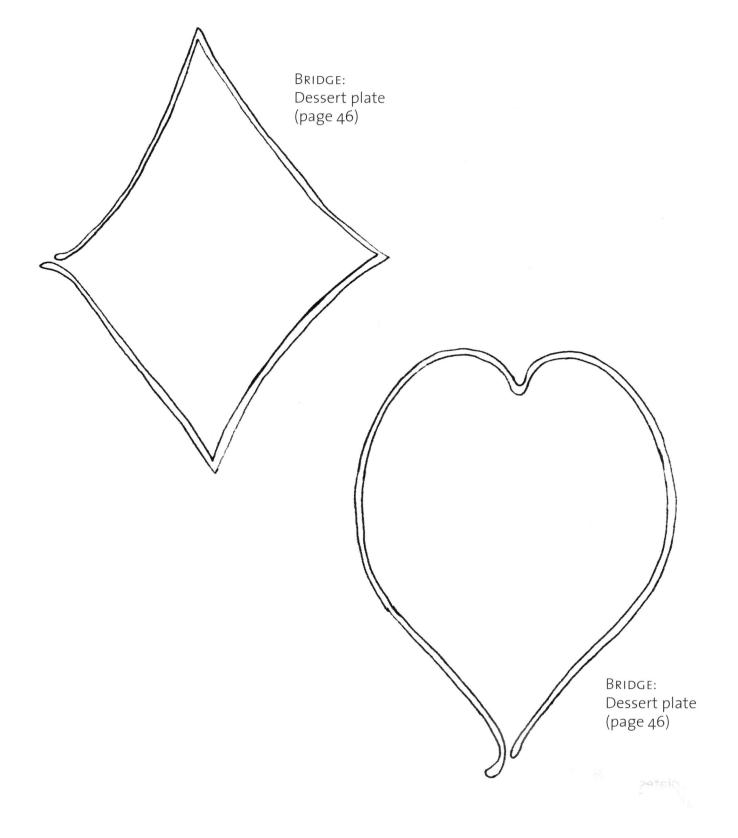

BRIDGE:
Dessert plate
(page 46)

BRIDGE:
Dessert plate
(page 46)

GINGERBREAD:
Biscuit tray and plates
(pages 52-53)

LEAVES:
Dinner plate
(page 56)

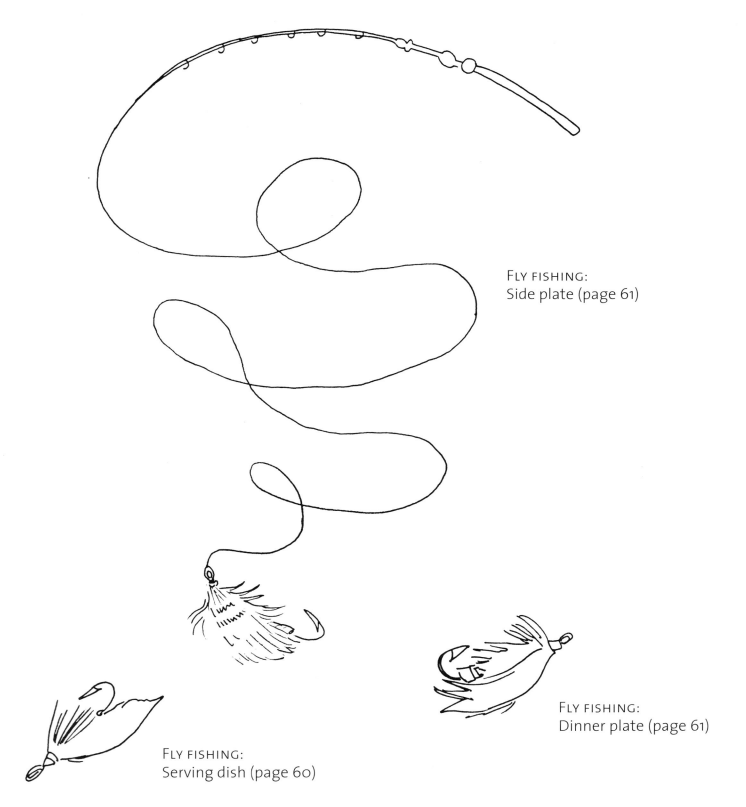

FLY FISHING:
Side plate (page 61)

FLY FISHING:
Serving dish (page 60)

FLY FISHING:
Dinner plate (page 61)

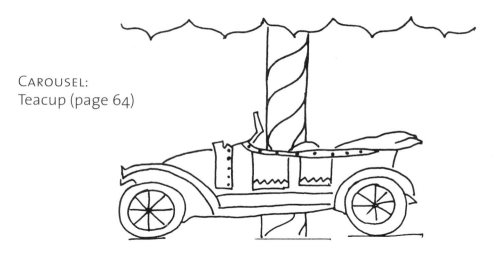

CAROUSEL:
Teacup (page 64)

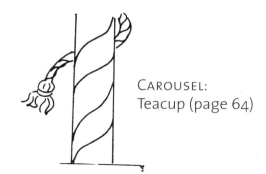

CAROUSEL:
Teacup (page 64)

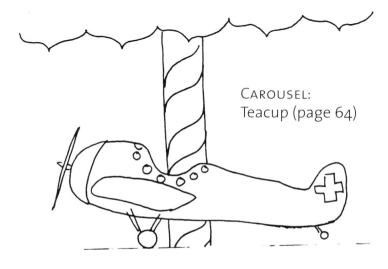

CAROUSEL:
Teacup (page 64)

CAROUSEL:
Teacup (page 64)

CAROUSEL:
Teacup (page 64)

CAROUSEL:
Teacup (page 64)

Carousel:
Tart dish (page 67)

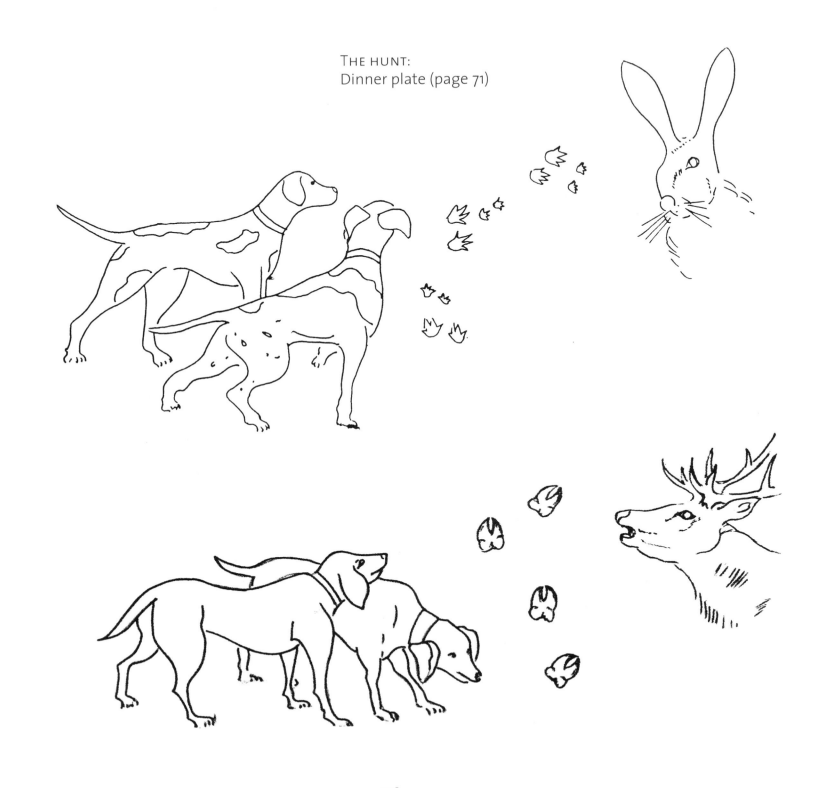

THE HUNT:
Dinner plate (page 71)

THE HUNT:
Dinner plate (page 71)

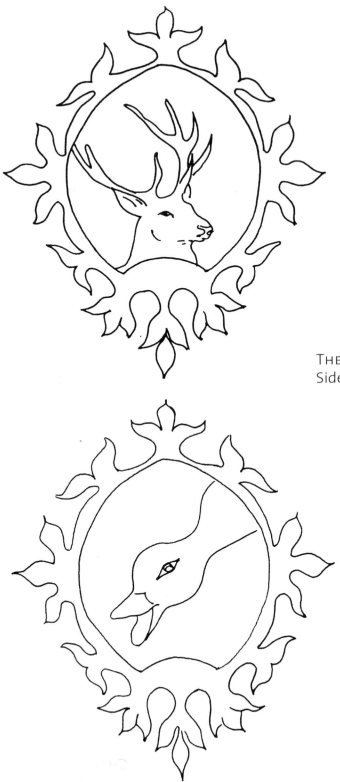

THE HUNT:
Side plate (page 72)

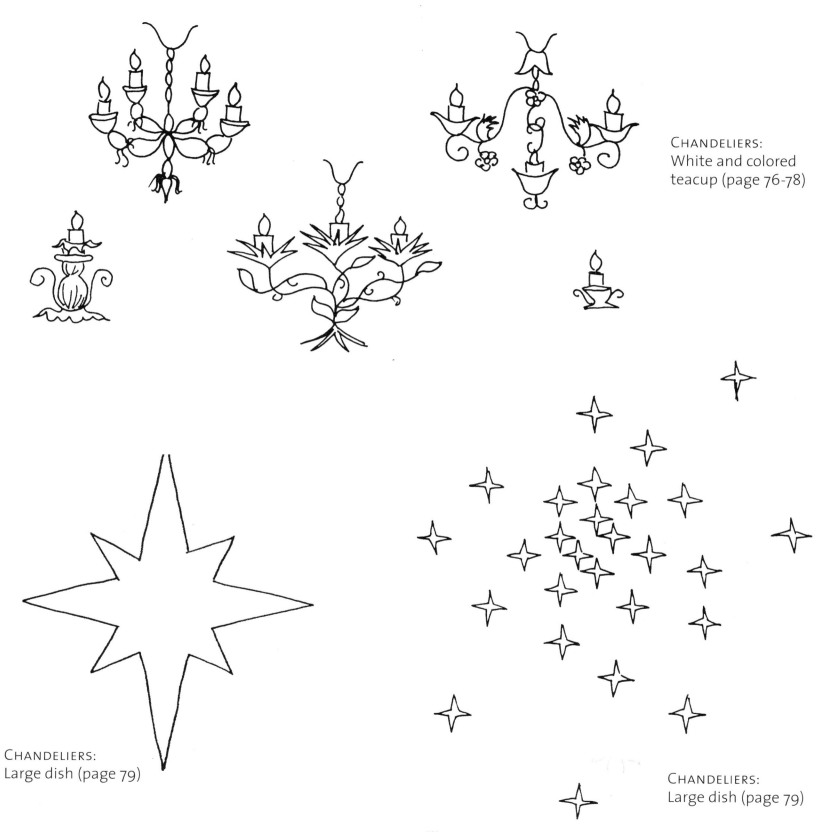

CHANDELIERS:
White and colored
teacup (page 76-78)

CHANDELIERS:
Large dish (page 79)

CHANDELIERS:
Large dish (page 79)

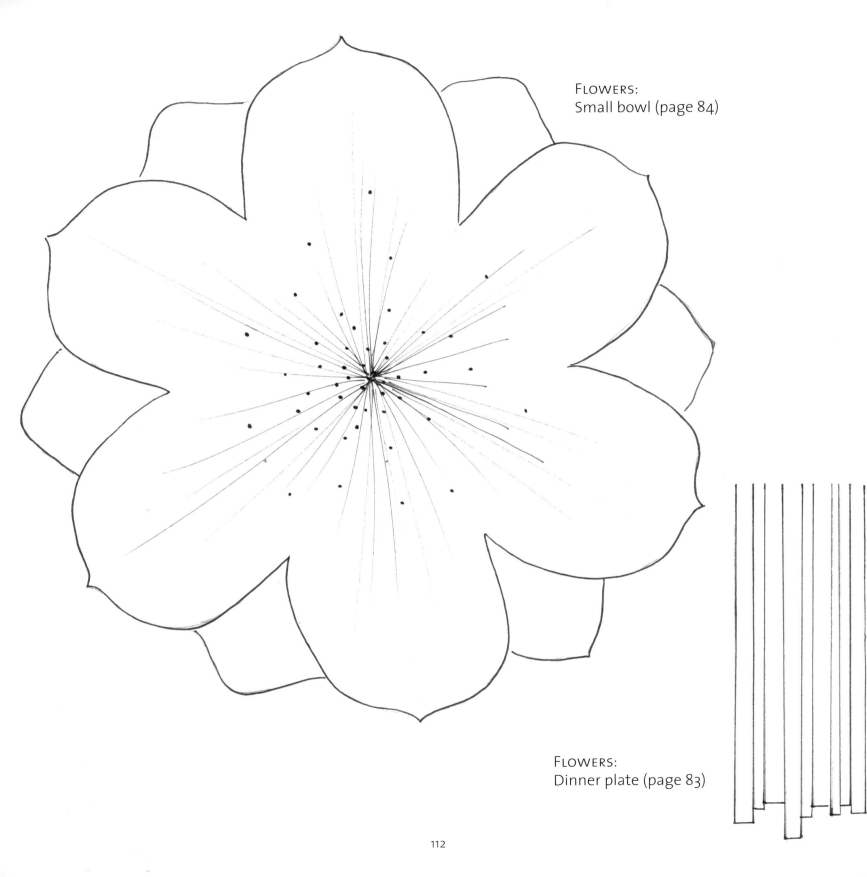

FLOWERS:
Small bowl (page 84)

FLOWERS:
Dinner plate (page 83)